A First Book of
MOZART

EXPANDED EDITION

David Dutkanicz

DOVER PUBLICATIONS
Garden City, New York

All music available as downloadable MP3s!

Go to www.doverpublications.com/0486849023
to access these files.

Dedicated to Peter and Anna

Bibliographical Note

A First Book of Mozart Expanded Edition is a revised and enlarged
republication of *A First Book of Mozart*, first published by Dover in 2005.

International Standard Book Number

ISBN-13: 978-0-486-84902-7
ISBN-10: 0-486-84902-3

Manufactured in the United States of America
84902301
www.doverpublications.com

2 4 6 8 10 9 7 5 3 1
2021

Contents

Works are arranged in order of approximate difficulty, with exceptions made to facilitate page turns.

Introduction

It is a mistake to think that the practice of my art has
become easy to me. I assure you, dear friend, no one
has given so much care to the study of composition as I.
There is scarcely a famous master in music whose works
I have not frequently and diligently studied.
—Wolfgang Amadeus Mozart (1756–91)

The present edition of *A First Book of Mozart* brings the joys of Mozart's music to beginning pianists. These carefully selected and arranged works are designed to develop both hands and ears as well as introduce the composer's more memorable masterpieces. Most of the works focus on special skills, such as double octaves and syncopation in the opening of Symphony No. 25 and melodic imitation in "Minuet in D." Fingerings are provided as suggestions. Since each set of hands plays differently, teachers and students are the best judges of what works. Earlier pieces have phrasing and pedaling left open. They can be filled in as the student progresses.

The aim of this edition is to help the beginning pianist grow to an intermediate level using the appropriate repertoire. Starting with the third movement of Piano Sonata No. 8 (on page 38), the arrangements encompass more of the original material. Phrasing is slowly introduced, as are more voices and notes per hand. The later piano works are presented in their original keys so that performers do not have to relearn music when they advance to the complete versions. MP3 recordings are available as downloads and serve as a guide.

Allegro

from Eine Kleine Nachtmusik

This is the opening of one of Mozart's most famous works, *Eine Kleine Nachtmusik*, which means "A Little Night Music." It was composed in 1787, when Mozart was living in Vienna. Be sure to keep the music light and flowing.

Allegro

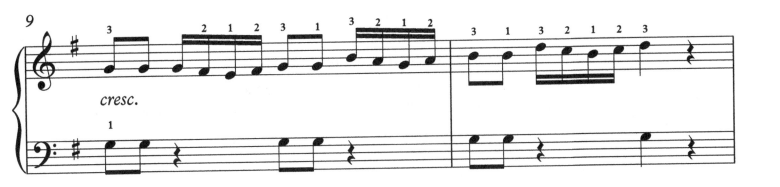

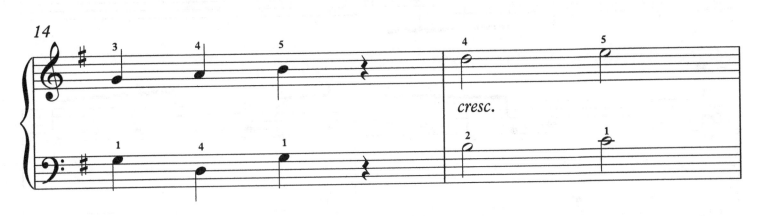

Romanze

from Eine Kleine Nachtmusik

Here is the second movement of *Eine Kleine Nachtmusik*. Altogether, there are four movements. Mozart spoke of a fifth, but unfortunately it is lost. The mood should be a bit calmer, in contrast to the lively first movement.

Andante

Minuet

from Don Giovanni

A minuet is a slow and stately dance in 3/4 time. This minuet is from one of Mozart's most famous operas, *Don Giovanni*. The characters all dance to the lovely melody.

Papageno's Song

from The Magic Flute

Not all operas are serious and stuffy. Mozart's *The Magic Flute* is a fairy-tale opera with a prince, a girl to be rescued, a wizard, and a comical bird catcher dressed in feathers called Papageno. "Yes, I am the bird catcher," he sings, "always cheerful, well-known everywhere! If only I could catch a sweet young girl so that she could be all mine!"

Light and lively

Serenade

from Don Giovanni

A serenade is a song of love. In olden times, it was performed under someone's window at night, with romantic moonlight in the background. This serenade from *Don Giovanni* is sung by the main character to his love. Play as if you were singing along.

Allegretto

Andante

from Piano Concerto No. 21

This is one of Mozart's most popular melodies, taken from Piano Concerto No. 21. Ever since it was played in a movie, it's gained the nickname "Elvira Madigan." Play gracefully, and give the two notes with sharps an extra push.

Andante

Romanze

from Piano Concerto No. 20

Mozart wrote twenty-seven piano concerti—the first in 1767, when he was only eleven years old! This famous melody is from the second movement of Piano Concerto No. 20. You may have heard this melody before.

Andante

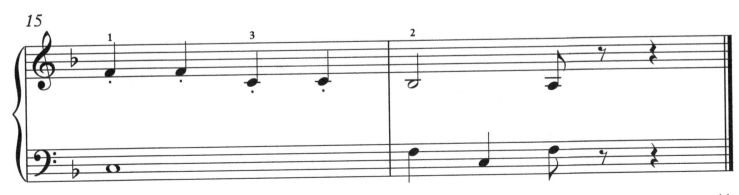

Sleigh Ride

from Three German Dances

"Sleigh Ride" is the third of *Three German Dances*, which Mozart composed in 1791. Originally for orchestra, the piece contains repeated notes that remind us of jingling sleigh bells. The melody in the right hand is like a bumpy ride through the snow.

Allegro

Trio

from Three German Dances

Another theme from *Three German Dances* is this trio. A trio is usually the second melody in a dance. Keep the mood light and lively, just like a dance.

Minuet in C

This charming minuet comes from *Nannerl's Notebook*, a collection of small pieces named after the composer's older sister. Amazingly, these pieces were composed when Mozart was only six years old. They were his first works to be published.

Moderato

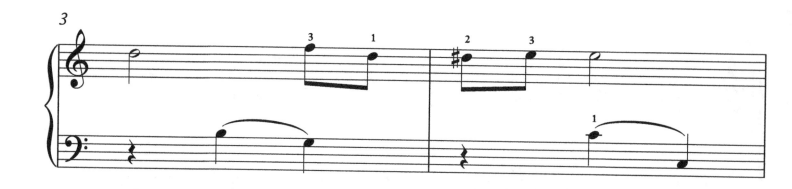

Aria

from Don Giovanni

Here is another piece from *Don Giovanni*—this time an aria. Sung by a solo voice, an aria allows a character to express thoughts and feelings uninterrupted. You might want to hum or sing along!

Overture

to The Marriage of Figaro

An overture is an introduction to an opera, where the main themes are introduced and the story is outlined—much like a movie trailer. This overture is from *The Marriage of Figaro*, where the story is more like a soap opera. Figaro is set to marry his love, Susanna, only to have an old count return and try to steal her away. This overture sets the tone for the lively story.

Presto

Twinkle Twinkle Little Star

with Variation

The original title is "Ah, vous dirai-je, Maman," which means "Ah, Mother, if I could tell you." Follow the notes closely, as the original is a little different from what you may be used to. Mozart used this song to teach, and he wrote a set of Twelve Variations on the theme.

Moderato

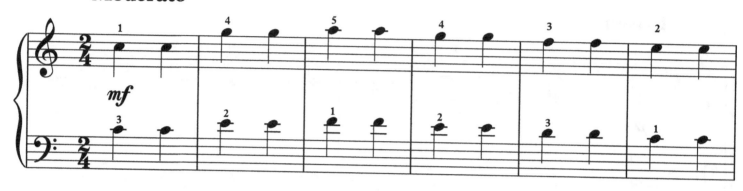

Variation

Lullaby

This lullaby was originally written for voice and piano. The opening words are "Never a sound does arise. Everyone slumbering lies." Be sure to play gently and follow the dynamics.

Moderato

Andante

from Piano Sonata No. 11

Mozart wrote nineteen sonatas for piano, and this is the opening theme of Piano Sonata No. 11. The melody is very elegant, as indicated by the tempo marking, *andante grazioso* ("at a gracefully walking pace").

Andante grazioso

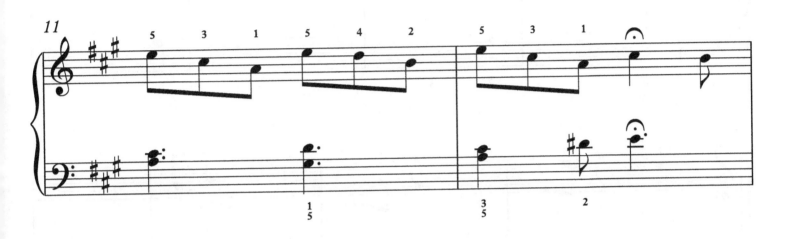

Lento

from Clarinet Concerto

In Mozart's time, the clarinet was a brand-new instrument; it was not widely known. His concerto was the first of its kind and made the clarinet a popular instrument. Remember that a clarinetist needs to breathe. Shape your phrases as if you were breathing along to the music.

Lento

Aria

from The Marriage of Figaro

Here is an aria from *The Marriage of Figaro*. One of the characters compares his love to a butterfly and promises to "never let her fly away again." Listen to how Mozart paints the image of a butterfly flying and landing by having the melody rise up and then flutter back down.

Tempo di marcia

Glockenspiel

from The Magic Flute

This piece is from *The Magic Flute*. In this scene, Papageno, the feathered bird catcher, appears onstage and plays magical bells that make grumpy people happy again. Play the notes brightly, as if you were playing the bells and making grumpy people happy.

Allegro moderato

Minuet in D

Mozart wrote many minuets. He was so proficient that he created a game for which he would write minuets by rolling dice! In this example, the right and left hands trade phrases. Look for the imitation, and try to create an echo.

Lively, but not too fast

Allegro

from Horn Concerto No. 2

This theme is taken from the last movement of Mozart's Horn Concerto No. 2. The horn was widely used at hunting events, where it would play special calls at the beginning and end of a meet. Play the piece with the same energy and excitement.

Moderato

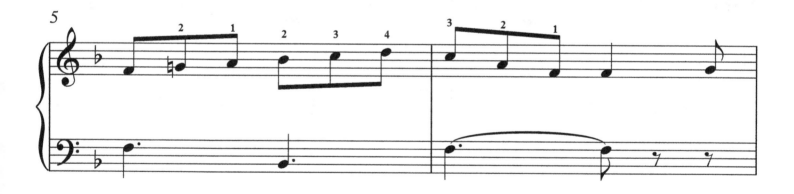

Rondo Alla Turca

This well-known melody is from the third movement of Piano Sonata No. 11. (The first movement is on page 22.) The notes can be tricky. Be sure to keep a nice and even pace, contrasting the *piano* and *forte* sections.

Allegretto

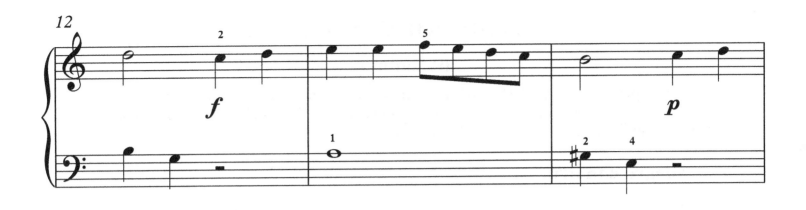

Symphony No. 25

(Opening)

This is the opening to one of Mozart's most famous symphonies. The notes are far apart in the beginning so that the piano can have a nice, big sound, almost like a full orchestra. Try to hear the strings playing the crisp syncopation in the beginning.

Allegro con brio

Symphony No. 40

(Opening)

Mozart wrote forty-one symphonies, and this was his second to last. He wrote over six hundred pieces before he tragically died at thirty-five. We can only imagine how many wonderful symphonies and other pieces he might have composed if he had lived longer.

Moderato

Piano Sonata No. 8

(Opening)

The opening theme to Piano Sonata No. 8 is a lively *allegro maestoso*, meant to be played "quickly and majestically." Like some other selections, this work is in a minor key. Contrast the *piano* and *forte* sections, and contrast the major and minor tonalities.

Allegro maestoso

Piano Sonata No. 8

Movement III

This lively *presto* is the third movement of Piano Sonata No. 8. Notice an alternate fingering in the right hand in the opening bar. Feel free to use either one. When you are comfortable, work up to a brisk tempo.

Menuet

from String Quartet No. 13

In addition to being a brilliant composer and pianist, Mozart was a very skilled violinist. He frequently performed chamber music with his friends. He composed twenty-six string quartets, with this menuet coming from the thirteenth.

Moderato

Voi Che Sapete

from The Marriage of Figaro

"Voi Che Sapete" is a popular aria from *The Marriage of Figaro*. It is sung in the second act by Cherubino, a young page who has fallen in love with the countess of the castle. He sings, "You know what love is . . . see whether it's in my heart. . . . It is new to me, and I do not understand it."

Moderato

Domine Deus

from Great Mass in C Minor

Of the fifteen settings of the Mass composed by Mozart, this one was the most celebrated and dubbed "Great." In measures five and six, take note of the thirds in the right hand. These may be tricky, especially using fingers three and five. Isolate these small examples, and practice them separately until they sound as smooth as the rest of the music.

Allegro moderato

Ave Verum Corpus

"Ave Verum Corpus" ("Hail, True Body") is a motet—a short, independent vocal work not connected to any other movements. It was composed only six months before Mozart's untimely passing. Although the number of voices varies between two and four, they should mimic a choir and sound as one.

Piano Concerto No. 7

(Opening)

Mozart composed this elegant concerto for orchestra and three solo pianos after being commissioned to write it for a countess and her two daughters. He rearranged it as a more practical two-piano version, which has become the standard performance practice for this work. Pay attention to the contrast in dynamics as the rhythmic opening changes into a more lyrical passage at measure four.

Piano Concerto No. 15

Movement III

In a letter to his father, Mozart described this concerto as a work that would "make one sweat" due to its technical demands. In this movement, the theme takes on a countryside characteristic. Beginning in measure nine, pay close attention to the octaves in the right hand. Use the single notes (e.g., F in measure ten) as an opportunity to reposition your hand and prepare for the next phrase of octaves.

Piano Sonata No. 1

(Opening)

Mozart composed his first full piano sonata in 1774, at the age of eighteen. Notice a wavy line in front of the right-hand chord at the beginning in measures one, three, five, and seven. This is known as an *arpeggio* line—the notes should be rolled up, starting from the bottom.

Allegro

Piano Concerto No. 2

Movement II

Many of Mozart's early piano concerti were inspired by contemporary composers whom he admired. This movement is based on original melodies from a sonata by John Schobert (c. 1720–67). The playful opening is followed by a long series of triplets, which need to be played evenly. Use the quarter notes in the left hand to help keep the tempo evenly metered.

Andante

Piano Concerto No. 23

(Opening)

This piano concerto was composed in 1786, shortly before the premiere of *The Marriage of Figaro*. It is an elegant work and considered part of Mozart's mature phase. Play the heartfelt melody evenly, adding pedal when appropriate to sustain the *dolce* ("sweet") character beginning in measure eight.

Piano Concerto No. 5

Movement II

Mozart adds a unique tempo marking to the second movement of this concerto: *andante ma un poco adagio* ("at a walking pace but slightly slow"). Play at a comfortable tempo, but be careful not to drag out the melody. Do not use too much pedal, as the music can become murky and block out melodic movement.

Andante ma un poco adagio

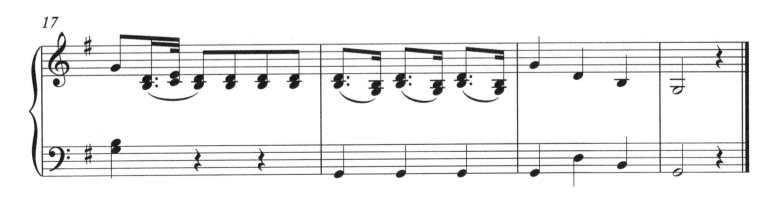

Piano Sonata No. 7

Movement III

The left-hand patterns in this sonata are quite common in the Classical period and are known as an *Alberti bass*, named after Domenico Alberti, who popularized the technique in the early 1700s. It serves two purposes: to outline harmony and simultaneously supply a rhythmic pulse. Keep the left hand in the background, and use it to support the melodic material of the right hand.

Allegretto grazioso

Piano Concerto No. 9

Movement II

This work was written for Victoire Jenamy, the daughter of famous ballet master Jean-Georges Noverre. It is known as the "Jenamy" concerto in her honor, although the concerto is also referred to as the "Jeunehomme." Before playing, review the key signature (three flats) and practice the parallel-third passages in the left hand (measures eight and ten) separately until they are smooth.

Piano Sonata No. 16

Movement I (Excerpt)

Mozart composed this sonata specifically for beginners, and it is also known as the "Sonata Facile" ("Easy Sonata"). Scales play an important role in this work and should be practiced beforehand. Review the grace notes in measure twenty-two and the trill in measure twenty-five. They serve an ornamental purpose and should not detract from the music.

(turn page)

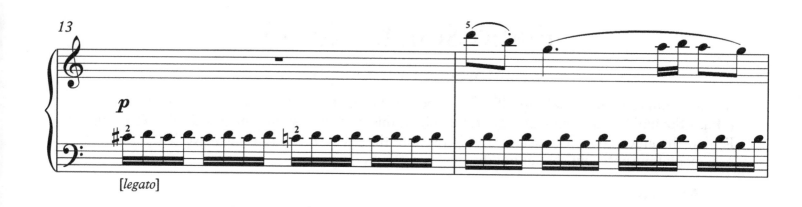

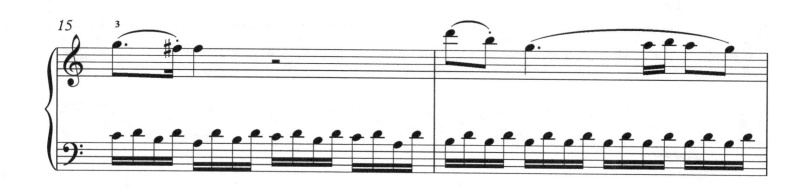

Fantasie in D Minor

(Excerpt)

A *fantasie* refers to a composition that is improvisatory and does not strictly follow any musical forms. It was left unfinished at the time of Mozart's passing, with the final bars filled in by German composer August Eberhard Müller. Perform each of the three sections distinctly, and keep the final section unhurried.

(turn page)